Contents

KU-506-957

HOT AIR BALLOONING

Keith West

Published in association with The Basic Skills Agency

Hodder & Stoughton

A MEMBER OF THE HODDER HEADLINE GROUP

Acknowledgements
Cover: Photodisc Blue

Photos: p. 2 © London Aerial Photo Library/CORBIS; p. 7 © Peter Finger/CORBIS; p. 13 © Hulton-Deutsch Collection/CORBIS; p. 18 © Washington University/CORBIS SYGMA; p. 22 © The Press Association Ltd 2001; p. 26 © S. Feval/ Le Matin/CORBIS SYGMA.

Every effort has been made to trace copyright holders of material reproduced in this book. Any rights not acknowledged will be acknowledged in subsequent printings if notice is given to the publisher.

Orders: please contact Bookpoint Ltd, 130 Milton Park, Abingdon, Oxon OX14 4SB. Telephone (44) 01235 827720, Fax: (44) 01235 400454. Lines are open from 9.00–6.00, Monday to Saturday, with a 24 hour message answering service. You can also order through our website www.hodderheadline.co.uk

British Library Cataloguing in Publication Data
A catalogue record for this title is available from the British Library

ISBN 0 340 87310 8

First published 2003
Impression number   10 9 8 7 6 5 4 3 2 1
Year   2009 2008 2007 2206 2005 2004 2003

Typeset by SX Composing DTP, Rayleigh, Essex.
Printed in Great Britain for Hodder & Stoughton Educational, a division of Hodder Headline, 338 Euston Road, London NW1 3BH by Bath Press Ltd, Bath.

1 Up and Away!

Have you wanted to travel in a hot air balloon?
Think about climbing into the basket.
You might want to look up at the sky.
You might enjoy floating upwards.
You might want to be in the clouds.

Think about the heat and noise of the burners.
Burners are used in flight.
They heat the air in the balloon.
The hot air keeps the balloon up.

You will soon be up in the cold air.
You will wish you were wrapped up warm.
Some people wear gloves and scarves.
They also wear thick coats.

The views will be good.
You will see roads, trees and houses.

Hot air balloons give great views.

The balloon basket is full of sand bags.
The pilot can make the balloon rise higher.
He will throw out some sand bags.
The balloon will be lighter.
It will float upwards.

Perhaps you want to land?
The pilot will open a vent to let hot air escape.
Soon the balloon will gently fall to the earth.

Today, it is not difficult to ride
in a hot air balloon.
There are millions of
hot air balloons.
They come in all shapes and sizes.

There are plenty of people willing
to take you up, providing you have the money.

Men had always dreamed of flying.
Nobody had flown in any machine
until 1783.

How was it possible to fly in
a hot air balloon?
Who thought of the idea?

2 All About Hot Air Balloons

If you are going to have a ride
in a hot air balloon,
you might want to
know if it is safe.
You might want to know what
hot air balloons are made of.

The balloon envelope
is made of a fabric called
rip-stop nylon.

The fabric is lightweight.
It is very strong.
It is coated on the inside.
The coating stops leaks.

The balloon basket is made of rattan.
Each basket is woven by hand.

When inflating the balloon
it is important to follow a procedure.

This is what happens.
The envelope is stretched
out on the ground.
It is then fixed to the basket.
The basket is usually
lying on its side.

A small fan blows air
into the balloon.
The fan is powered
by gasoline.

The burner is then turned on.
The air in the balloon is heated.
The hot air rises.
This lifts the balloon upright.

Four people help to get
the balloon inflated.
On gusty and windy days,
more than four people are needed.

You cannot steer
a hot air balloon.
It goes where the
wind takes it.

Wind blows in different directions.
Wind blows at different speeds.
It depends upon how high you are,
or how low you are.

Experienced pilots climb up
or go down in the air.
They try to make sure the
balloon takes them the
way they want to go.
They do not always succeed.

You will probably see balloons
in the sky just after sunrise.
Or you may see balloons
two hours before sunset.

This is when the wind is calm
and the air is stable.
This is when it is best to fly
a hot air balloon.

A hot air balloon at sunset.

A record for the
highest flying balloon is
19,811 metres.

Most balloons fly at 150–300 metres
above the ground.

Balloons carry fuel for
two hour flights.
Hot air balloons use propane.
When the burner valves open,
the propane gas is lit by a
pilot light in the burner.

Sometimes a flame shoots out.
It can shoot as high as 6 metres
into the air.

Balloons cannot go back to
where they started from.

A chase crew follow the balloon.
They drive a recovery vehicle.
The crew are needed to
help the passengers
when the balloon lands.

3   Early Ballooning History

Most people think Joseph Montgolfier
invented the hot air balloon.
He was French.
He was born in 1740.
Joseph was full of ideas.

The French went to
war with Britain.
Britain owned Gibraltar.

Nobody could invade Gibraltar.
It was protected by land and sea.

Joseph was sitting
in front of a fireplace.
He wondered how the French
could invade Gibraltar.

His wife wanted to dry her nightdress.
She hung it near the fireplace to dry quickly.
Smoke and heat from the fire
filled up her nightdress.
The nightdress floated up to the ceiling.

Joseph realised how Gibraltar
could be attacked.

It could be attacked
from the air by
hot air balloons.
French soldiers could sit in
the balloons and
attack the British soldiers on the ground.

Joseph made a giant paper bag.
He made gas by burning
wet straw and chopped wool.
The gas sent
the bag 30 metres into the air.

Joseph and his brother
made a large envelope.
They wrapped it with fabric.
They held it together with 2,000 buttons.

On 4 June 1783,
they tried to fly the bag.

Several men held
the balloon down.
They burned
straw and wool.

The balloon filled with gas.
The men let the balloon go.
It flew 1,981 metres into the sky.

Joseph decided to
try a manned flight.

The King of France watched.

The balloon flew for 20 minutes.
It got up to 914 metres.
It landed safely.

The King of France clapped.

Gibraltar never was attacked
by French soldiers in hot air balloons.

4 Balloon Races

By now the Americans
and British flew balloons.

The first balloon race
was held in 1906.
It was called the
Coup Gordon Bennett race.

People still say 'Gordon Bennett'.
The phrase probably comes from this race.

The winner of the race was
the person who could fly
his balloon the furthest
non-stop.

The first winner was an American,
Frank Lahm.

The Gordon Bennett Balloon Race, 1938.

The first manned balloon
race to the stratosphere
was in 1932.
August Piccard
flew his balloon
up to 16,000 metres.
Piccard was the first person
to fly in a pressurised capsule
on a balloon flight.

An altitude record
was set in 1935.
'Explorer 11' climbed
to 22,066 metres.

It proved humans can
survive at very high altitudes.

5 Modern-Day Ballooning

In 1960, a man named Ed Yost
flew the first modern
hot air balloon.
It was made in America.

The first Atlantic crossing by a
hot air balloon was
on 12 August 1978.
The pilots set off from
Maine Island in America.
They landed in France.
The balloon was called
'Double Eagle 11'.

The first Trans-Pacific
balloon crossing
was from Japan to California.

Soon men dreamed about
flying around the world
in a hot air balloon.

The first men to try were
Maxi Anderson and Don Ida.
They started out in Egypt
on 11 January 1981.

The balloon came down
two days later.
It came down in India.

Maxi and Don had failed
but the dream lived on.

6 Floating Around the World

A prize was announced.
The winner would be the
first balloon to float
around the world
without stopping.

Steve Fossett
built a balloon.
He called her
'Solo Spirit'.
She was launched
from Argentina
on 7 August 1998.

She managed to float
a great distance.
She got as far as
the Pacific Ocean.

Steve Fossett in 'Solo Spirit'.

On 16 August,
a terrible storm blew up.
'Solo Spirit' was hit by lightning.
She fell 8,839 metres.
She hit the ocean.

She was 805 kilometres
from Australia.

Steve Fossett was still alive.
He called for help and
he was rescued.

'Solo Spirit' set a
new distance record.
The record was 22,909 kilometres.

Steve wondered if he would
ever try again.
He had been close to death.

He did try again.
He tried with Richard Branson
and Per Linstrand.

Another balloonist wanted
to win the prize.
Richard Branson had
decided to try.

Richard Branson had
grown rich with
Virgin Records.
He could afford
to build balloons.

He wanted to be
the first person to
float around the world
in a hot air balloon.

Could he do it?

7 The Virgin Global Challenges

The Virgin Global Challenge
started in 1998.
Per Lindstrand
and Steve Fossett
joined Richard Branson.

The 'Virgin Global Challenger'
flew over the Pacific ocean.
It looked as if they would
be the first to fly
around the world.

Then a trough of air stopped
the balloon's progress.
The crew had to ditch
16 kilometres north of Hawaii.
The crew were rescued
without being in danger.

Per Linstrand, Steve Fossett and Richard Branson in the
'Virgin Global Challenger'.

Richard Branson
did not give up.
He decided to try again in May 1999.

Richard thought the odds
were against anyone succeeding.
But he would still have fun trying.

The problem is that balloons
cannot be tested before
they fly around the world.

Things have not always
gone to plan for Richard.

He has had a fire on board.

He had to push the balloon upwards.
The balloon had to climb 14,325 metres.
It had to climb quickly.
Fire cannot burn where
the air is thin.

If the balloon had not climbed
14,325 metres then Richard
and his crew might have
burned to death.

Richard and his crew have also
faced terrible snowstorms.
They met the snowstorms
over the Rocky Mountains.

The storms were so bad
planes were diverted.
Even helicopters
could not get through.
Somehow, the balloon got through.

The Branson team try to
avoid landing in the sea.
The sea can be dangerous.

Sometimes they have no idea
where they might land.
It all depends upon the wind.

The 'Virgin Global Challenger' failed.
Richard Branson and his crew
failed to take the prize money.

They would not be the first to fly
around the world in
a hot air balloon.

8 An Amazing Achievement

Bertrand Piccard and Brian Jones
set off in their balloon,
'Breitling Orbiter 3',
on 1 March 1999.
They flew from the Swiss Alps.

Twenty days later
they had made it.
They touched down
on 20 March 1999.
They landed in Egypt.

The British Prime Minister, Tony Blair,
called the achievement fantastic.

The two men broke three records.
They had broken the distance record.
They had broken the duration record.
And they had floated around the world.

The 'Breitling Orbiter 3' on its world tour.

9 What Now?

Balloon racing is not over.
Balloonists now want to
break the records set
by the Breitling team.

Steve Fossett wanted to
be the first person
to fly around the world solo.

Steve took his balloon to Western Australia.
His new balloon was again named
'Solo Spirit'.

The balloon took off on 4 August 2001.
Steve was in the air for
12 days and 12 hours.
He didn't make it round the world,
but 'Solo Spirit' had been in the air
longer than any other solo balloon.
Steve had travelled 20,417 kilometres.

There will be more record attempts.

What about you?

Would you like to
be part of a team to float
around the world in
a hot air balloon?

Or would you like to try flying solo?

Are you willing to risk
your life on a
great adventure?

Are you up for it?

Somebody will be.
Somebody will break
more records in a hot air balloon.

Why not you?